# SLATE



Earth's Rocks

Tracy Vonder Brink

Norwood House Press

**Cataloging-in-Publication Data**

Names: Vonder Brink, Tracy.
Title: Slate / Tracy Vonder Brink.
Description: Buffalo, NY : Norwood House Press, 2027. | Series: Earth's rocks | Includes glossary and index.
Identifiers: ISBN 9781978580206 (pbk.) | ISBN 9781978580213 (library bound) | ISBN 9781978580220 (ebook)
Subjects: LCSH: Metamorphic rocks--Juvenile literature. | Metamorphism (Geology)--Juvenile literature. | Rocks--Juvenile literature.
Classification: LCC QE475.A2 V66 2027 | DDC 552.4--dc23

Published in 2027 by
**Norwood House Press**
2544 Clinton Street
Buffalo, NY 14224


Designer: Rhea Magaro
Editor: Kim Thompson

Photo credits: Cover, p. 1 Thorsten Schier/Shutterstock.com; p. 3 EVGEIIA/Shutterstock.com; p. 4 Kavic.C/Shutterstock.com; p. 5 lucky_pics/Shutterstock.com; p. 6 MansurVashaev/Shutterstock.com; p. 7 Randi Grace Nilsberg/Shutterstock.com; p. 9 BlueRingMedia/Shutterstock.com; p. 10 VisualProduction/Shutterstock.com; p. 11 Jeremy Reschke/Shutterstock.com; p. 12 HiTecherZ/Shutterstock.com; p. 13 doolmsch/Shutterstock.com; p. 15 Uniteam/Shutterstock.com; p. 16 Laura Webb/Shutterstock.com; p. 18 Pavel1964/Shutterstock.com; p. 19 Wozzie/Shutterstock.com; p. 21 Sheila Say/Shutterstock.com;



Printed in the United States of America



CPSIA compliance information: Batch #CSNHP27: For further information contact Norwood House Press at 1-800-237-9932.

# TABLE OF CONTENTS

# WHAT IS SLATE?

Rocks make up many things in the world, from tall mountains to the deep seafloor. All rocks are made of **minerals**. They are put into three main groups based on how they form.

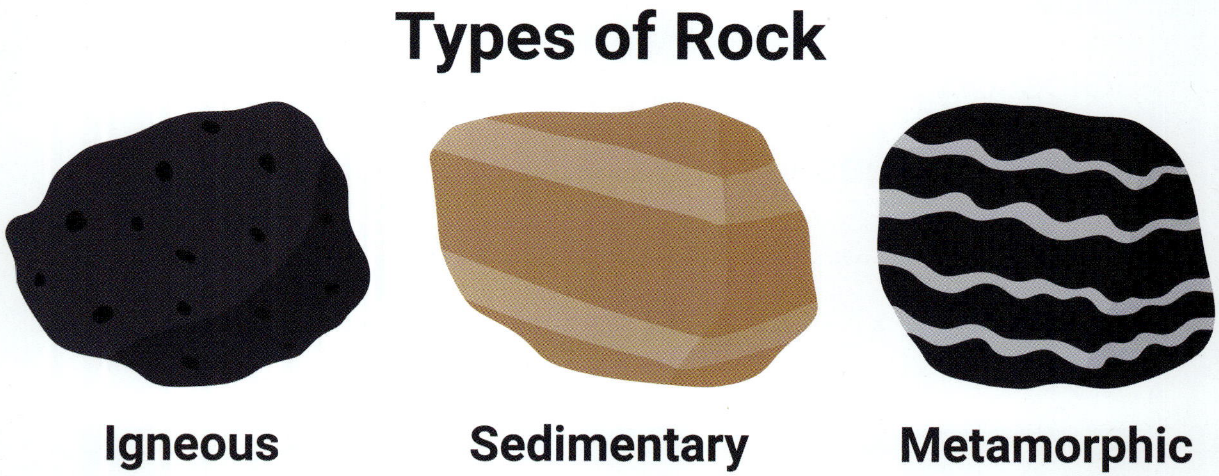

Metamorphic rocks start out as other rocks. The original rocks go through a **metamorphosis**. They change into a new kind of rock. Slate is a metamorphic rock.

Slate forms from sedimentary rocks like shale and mudstone. Heat and **pressure** below Earth's surface change these rocks into slate.

Slate comes in many colors. It can be black, blue, gray, red, green, or even purple.

# HOW DOES SLATE FORM?

Like all rocks, slate forms during Earth's rock cycle.

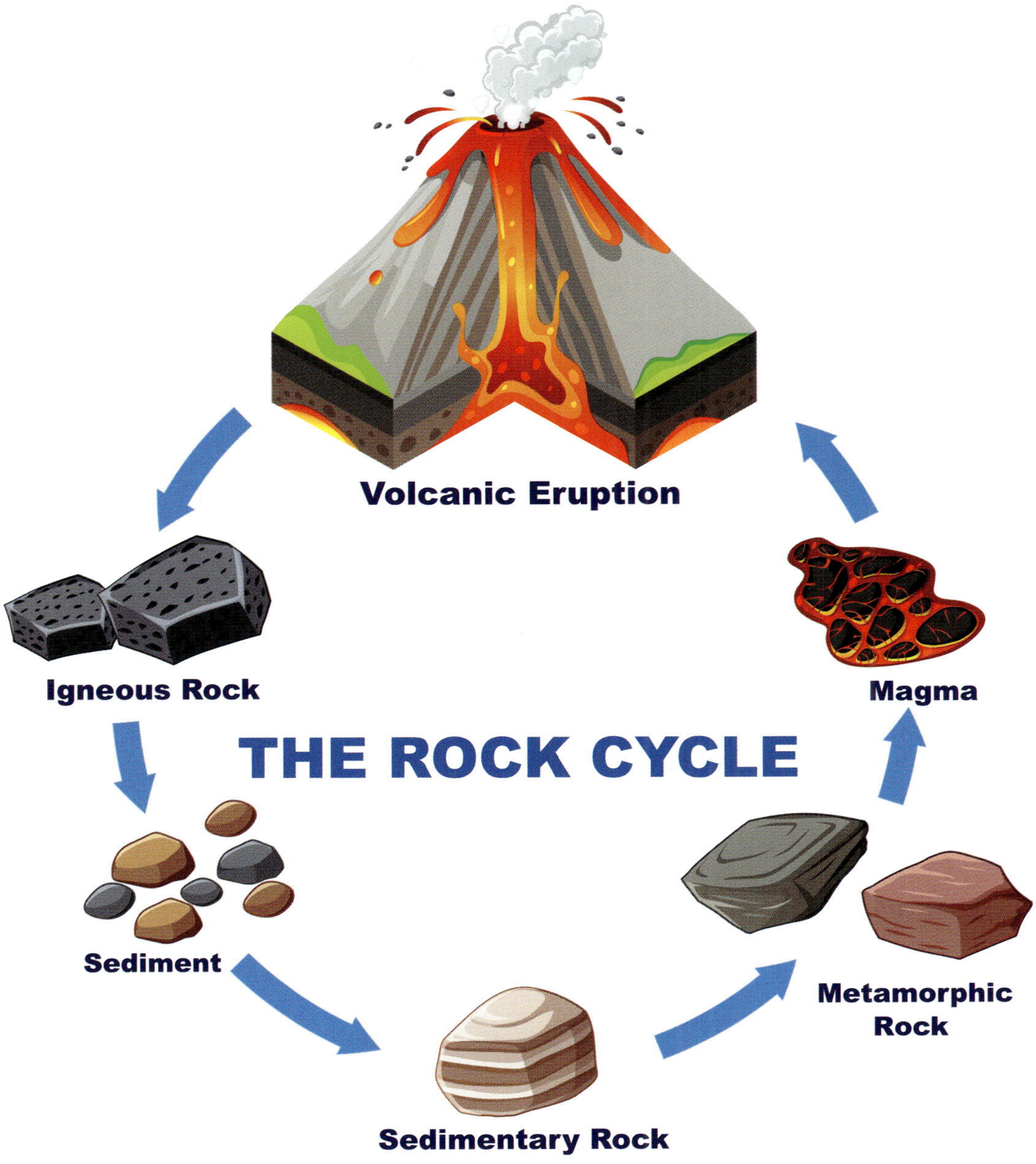
Volcanic Eruption
Igneous Rock
THE ROCK CYCLE
Magma
Sediment
Metamorphic
Rock
Sedimentary Rock

Earth has layers. The crust is the top layer. The crust is made up of huge pieces called **tectonic plates**. The plates move, even though we don't usually feel it.

Sometimes, plates run into each other. They push together so hard that they create lots of pressure. This can **uplift** rocks into mountains. It can also shove rocks deeper into Earth's crust.

Sometimes, shale and mudstone get pushed deep into Earth's crust. The pressure squashes minerals in the rocks. High temperatures in the crust also heat up the rocks.

The pressure and heat change the rocks' minerals. The rocks are no longer shale or mudstone. They become slate.

# WHERE IS SLATE FOUND?

Slate is found around the world in places where plates have crashed together. These places are often near mountains. Parts of North America, South America, Asia, and Europe have slate.

Slate Valley runs for about 24 miles (39 kilometers) between New York and Vermont in the United States. It's famous for having many different colors of slate. Slate has been **mined** here for over 100 years.

# HOW IS SLATE USED?

People have used slate for a long time. **Indigenous** groups in the Arctic used it to make tools. Students in the 1800s used slate tablets for school. They wrote on the slate with chalk and then wiped it off.

Slate is easy to cut into thin sheets. These are often used as roof **shingles**. Slices of slate also make good floors or garden paths. Some people even use slate as serving trays for cheese and other snacks.

Slate is found around the world. This common rock is easy to cut and use. If you look, you may find some covering your roof or your floor.

# GLOSSARY

**Indigenous** (in-DI-juh-nuhs): the first or earliest people to live in a place

**metamorphosis** (met-uh-MOR-fuh-sis): a complete or great change in appearance or form; a transformation

**mined** (mined): dug minerals from the ground

**minerals** (MIN-ur-uhlz): solids that form naturally in Earth and that do not come from an animal or plant; slate contains minerals such as quartz and mica

**pressure** (PRESH-ur): the weight or force of something pushing on something else

**shingles** (SHING-guhls): thin, flat pieces of wood, stone, or other material used to cover roofs

**tectonic plates** (tek-TAHN-ik playts): gigantic pieces of Earth's crust that fit together like puzzle pieces and that form continents and ocean floors

**uplift** (UP-lift): the raising of Earth's surface in response to natural causes

# THINKING QUESTIONS

1. How are rocks put into groups?
2. What rocks does slate come from?
3. What creates the pressure that makes slate?
4. Where is slate found?
5. Describe some of the ways people use slate.

# INDEX



# ABOUT THE AUTHOR


**Tracy Vonder Brink** is always curious about the world around her. She loves to make facts and true stories fun and has written many books for kids. Tracy lives near Cincinnati, Ohio, and enjoys reading, hiking, and playing with her two rescue dogs.